Disconnected Sonnets

R. Speegz

DEDICATION

To my Mom,
who is the first poet I've known.

CONTENTS

Life has been your art.
You have set yourself to music.
Your days are your sonnets.

Oscar Wilde

Earlier Sonnets

The painter
puts brush to canvas
and the poet
puts pen to paper.
The poet has the easier task,
for his pen does not alter
his rhyme.

Robert Brault

Leave-Taking, 2009

The haunting voice of the flute like herald will say--
The wings fluttering behind are inches away;
Pack of many tears falls in the rim of the eyes
And somber waits till the flute again calls, the wings flies.
The dulcet love songs of thy melancholic voice,
With the loud spoken strums and of its truest hues,
And the delicate touch of the paraded plucks,
Like violin will sing the highest in our hearts.
The keys are the keys to a masterpiece like you,
The pieces are the pieces of the glorious soul too.
The piano cannot be played for eternity,
Yet, the array of notes can be live infinitely.

The guitar may never be heard for many years,
The muse will always sing music that are yours...

The Shade, 2012

Hark, the aslant thin shade of the tree feisty
Takes heart to shed leaves of disguises,
Educing the sap --- forgotten, gloomy
No! there'll be flat no twists in the branches
Nor shakes of the trunk with the nosy wind
Eloquent, inexpectant to be, ere thee
But with earnest hopes, thou art confident;
Lest, not enough's the splendor of the tree,
Even might not, its very existence,
Rosily flourish with thy care utmost
Yearned not for thy green thumb, for it's useless,
Can't fruit their nods, nor thy smile cherished most.

Yet, the heartwood weeps and the inward tears
May replenish what lacks and wreck all fears.

Obssession, 2011

From the warm air you breathe, my world is lit
And I long for it long, well to dwell
But ends as a mere wish, only a pigment
Of my soaring phantasm; yes, unreal;
Because when I essay to cover us,
Everything in my touch dissolves to mist;
There's nothing left, neither debris or ash,
And even your footprints are gone amidst;
The warmth blows into its utmost coldness,
The same air is an eerie song itself
That seems covering the ears with seashells;
Seems closing the eyes is to see the thief.

But there's no really culprit, I knew
It's just my heart so deluded of you.

Square Room, 2012

There's no sound to hear in that small, square room
Where the long silence hints the skin fibers
Of the hundred hidden tales swung in doom
Like an old pendulum on midnight hours.
There's no motion to see in that chamber,
Except the sluggish dance of the dim tongue
Stretched by a thirsty lamp in one corner
And the thin smokes that are silently hung.
Scent of absent flowers floats in the air,
Touch of cold wind sends any spine shiver,
Taste of bittersweet memories come near,
Whirling inside one's tired mind over and over.

There's been no knock in the door ever since
Because that dark, small square room is death-dense.

Forgiveness, 2014

Not as swift as to ruin, to build and to mend are
And so do trusting and trusting back again;
It is not asked: not a question forgiveness is; nor
Begged, for an alm it is not. A gift it poses then,
For forgiveness is given, never by force but will:
A choice. This choice is a plain statement made from perplexed
Thoughts that wanted peace, freedom from all feelings of ill,
A new start with the same, or separate ways. Not fixed
Wholly when presented but installed; at times, a prize:
earned, not seized; won, through signs and test of sincerity.
But forgiveness recreates not, one should realize,
The past; makes the future without barring enmity.

Forgiving does not forget as forgetting does not
Forgive. Yet, it is remembering with hatred nought.

Fishing, 2014

Five times a big fish was angled to my hook
And five times did I throw one back at the river.
The species sought by me, merely in the book
Have I know and its fin have I seen closer.
Commonly will one hurt the net on fishes
Scaled with silver or gold, yet my hands aim not
What fills the basket, but what fills the wishes
Of my heart in deprivation near to rot.
Fisherman, merchants may tick about the net
Sewn with gaping holes called my brain – it is nix.
The union of brain and heart is hard to get
When it detaches from the mercantile bricks.

For the world is a keen spear, the heart should bleed,
Not with pain, but for the passion that doesn't yield.

Divergent Forks, 2014

In profound silence the cerebrum finds light between
The divergent forks of the road to self-fulfillment;
One grants freedom – to abandon, to venture, to preen;
The other ends the family's impoverishment;
Every path has payment, one can only be taken,
Either choice weighs both to gratitude and selfishness;
So which transpires the soul to be just but less broken?
Which also guarantees genuine happiness?
On mutualism hope of both feeds, to gain entrée
To the gate of comfort, to the fortress of fortune;
Whose aspirations be stood by at the end of day?
Whose toils are bitterer, worthy of fruition?

What are the parameters? Codes of comparison?
Show a detour instead that runs but one horizon.

Forbidding, 2013

Abruptly had frozen the still lagoon
By the touch of the of the icy breath of the air
Chinked frantically like a timed snare
To beat the bleak winds' endless, lazy drones;
The thin spray of mist solitude-laden
Threw off the scent of a forgotten grave,
Sending any nearby creature to grieve
And obliterating any haven;
Even the woods were weeping like willow
Seemed tired of jutting to the pitch-black sky:
No moon, no stars, merely a vacancy high,
Reflecting the great emptiness below.

What was befalling to this place idyllic
That once was always warm, safe, picturesque?

Series of Sonnets

The purpose of rhythm
it has always seemed to me,
is to prolong the moment
of contemplation –
the moment
when we are both asleep and awake,
which is the one moment
of creation –
by hushing us
with an alluring monotony,
while it holds us
waking by variety.

William Butler Yeats

Sonnet 1:00

Your first sonnet ever written was about a rose.
Along with a soft, stringed instrumental the gang
And you spoke its bud in unison. Why, who heard those
Waist-deep euphemisms, gave praise without discernment
Of the meanings left buried at the tip of the tongue?
Was it true; had it to be true as how did foment
By one unsung heroine amazed before you all?
Admiration! Open skin is admired; beneath
It is not understood. Perhaps, trick: a set of null!
Admiration! Is it naturally short-lived?
If your rose was admired, why lost like a babe teeth?
Now, you solely remember such red blossom waved.

Any chain of ornate words can be vague or vivid:
Few sing of it and fewer embrace its very seed.

Sonnet 2:00

There's no No when the throb of your heart throbs for your hand
And will you conduct the asked beat lief for her smile.
She's all the thoughts in your poetry and all her grand
Wish is the said poetry. So with a throbbing heart
Will you write in a paramour-confessing style,
Go talking about her adorable, you stalwart,
That you might be 'We'. So you give her your poetry
But it isn't enough; You pour your heart out but still,
It isn't enough. You present your kept chivalry
Although admitted it's not as battle-worn as his.
But again it is never enough that it can kill
You. Let her tell if she wants more or wants no more of this!

There's no No when the throb of your heart summons your soul
And there's no Yes even though you gave your all. O foul!

Sonnet 3:00

Somebody heard that a girl asked and was given,
Another did the same, then followed by several;
Thus given, too. With gladness to give, poem was woven
Expecting no huge cost, just gratitude and keeping
For every poem was sprung from sweat and blood and all.
You handed them; your mind was juvenile for doubting.
But when you asked them about the poem years later,
All but two told me that they had hidden it somewhere,
Implied: too lazy to comb, or had lost the paper.
Immediately had you made them because they wished so;
To idle, to ignore to forget is unfair.
The sole copy was what's given. You should've said no!

And now you've sworn not to let your poems perch like a dove
To anyone who is just curious but cannot love.

Sonnet 4:00

Breathe clean lungs of the tangled serpentine roads;
Let these breaths fly away with the magical structures
Sprouting atop each other at distance, or golds
And silvers of stars strewn on peaks and slopes at even.
With the natives and tourists, let the spirits capture
Inner peace harmonious to the serene haven.
Three hours by wheels, the pine city, found by lions
And admired by multitudes, towers the same throne
Ever-lofty and evergreen. By hearts of scions
For the life of their heavenly heritage, behold!
With clouds and magnificence, the vast mountains becrown;
Its preserved green fruitfulness and ancient culture, behold!

Climb the northern gate to paradise upper,
Where the world is viewed wider, the sky is seen closer.

Sonnet 5:00

Somewhere in September, for no reason at all,
You found you at the meanders of Summer Capital,
Skeltering with the cold wind like brittle leaves of Fall.
But the sluggish sorrow took flight, bypassing Winter;
You found you at the threshold of an accidental
Spring, in love with May, the season's pretty harbinger.
She is small, awkward and inclined to embonpoint
But she is full of intellect and spirits bubbling;
Unlike girls who dream to be a beautiful swan,
She lives with a heart to comfort the forgotten kids;
She loves the accordion and black coffee painting,
For on music and arts and charity her life feeds.

You found May, a classic flower in the torpid cold
And your frozen heart to blossom suddenly makes bold.

Sonnet 6:00

You drowse in the blurry point of view; your mind plunges
In her picture. You watch the mountains waltz in Kennon;
You heart dances fandango with hers in happiness.
In the cold breath of pine trees that touches your dry face
You remember your hands that touches her hair crimson,
You remember your hands entwined with yours. And it stays
In your chapping lips the sweet millisecond-swift kiss.
Her less but fast speeches, her black almond-shaped eyes,
Her love for algebra, her fear of praying mantis,
Her gray cat, her eleven-eleven, her story
From the crumpled and folded pages – all never dies
On your tongue. She is your most cherished strawberry.

In the twist of time and in a prank of the long drive
Your heart and the old bus suddenly jumps and off dive.

Sonnet 7:00

When the world spins and spins around like a bird frenzied,
There you stand in the midst of centripetal force,
Watching all colors dissolve into a wall misted.
Petrified as forest, nausea-overtaken,
Your soul splits up with indefinite ways to the course.
Fidgeting 'tween two spheres where clarity is shaven.
You are a lamp post astray on mid-road looking for light;
And you have grown roots through years of monotonous steps,
Seeping hope you're not a sunflower on endless night.
You are too old for a new-fangled pacifier
But, you think, too young to self-take doses of verbal peps
Lest your hands and feet are tied up with barbed wire.

The world won't stop spinning but soon on your hollowed palm,
But you must watch it fade until these troubled eyes calm.

Sonnet 8:00

Sprawled on a dusty mat, like a cockroach capitalizing the absent
Light, your body was quiet as the coarse hand of sleep
Pats with sarcasm. Pulsating with the effervescent
Mobile radio, your body was glued to whirling
Stained pictures from the air. Your body felt its own deep
Ghost who was in the alley of wishes wandering.
Repetitive wishes gloved the sleep with irony
While sleep surely spreads out dying enthusiasm.
Must you lay in between half-awake and half-asleep be?
Surely exhaustion will replace you; you'll be driven
To whichever state of mind. Those old wishes, toss'm!
Toss'm and get that missed sleep, not restless and broken.

You must keep what don't promise any fictitious good
Or what salt the wounds: twin of eternal brood.

Sonnet 9:00

If you're palsied by the many strikes of dilemmas,
Whether those strikes are in unison or in arrays,
Let your body fall but the heart. For it will be Was
And Were all the Is and Are that are piercing your soul.
If you're in coma by the vast pool of lonelies'
Thoughts, whether those thoughts to your life has long or deep role,
Let your mind sleep but the heart. Because it will be plain
And Just all the crux and superlative to you.
If you are cold dead in the heavy downpours of pain,
Lay still with your heart beside Him. Lay your heart to Him.
For all the sadness and tremors could He pound into
Dust, the same which you're molded in the likeness of Him.

Fear not. The macabre and tremendous are nothing for He.
Fear not. Fear not if in his hands your spirits be.

Sonnet 10:00

Gray Fellow, how do you twirl Time between your fingers?
Sometimes you come earlier than bird, sometimes later
Than a hare. Other times you come in the fretted curse
Expression of the clock. You're an uninvited guest
People must succumb even out of grudge o languor –
Whether just right, early or late is never perfect.
O, how do you survive with tell-by-chance piece of Time?
With your sweeping sickle to give a taste or the whole
Of Bitterness which has no other words that right-rhyme,
People tried to estimate and follow the rhythm
Of your step as to possibly obtain a parole
Or steal an extension in vain, grievance and mayh'm.

You're the irreversible loss all will surely meet;
You're the end pushing people to live to the limit.

Sonnet 11:00

Life is not a blank canvas which has to be drawn on
Nor the brush which has to be chosen by the best stroke.
It's not the palette holding the colors to be done
Nor the colors themselves that make up what's to be born.
It is not the image seen or reckoned that mind spoke
Nor the depiction wrought that's alive with hues it's worn.
Life is not the hand that maneuvers each tool and thought
Nor the inner juice encouraging the hand to move.
But life is the picturing of subject to be caught,
The picking of best paraphernalia and colors.
It's the flow of heart's yen, the movement of hands that wove,
The birthing of a splendor for the sake of splendors.

Life is not anything known to be stationary
But innate with action that creates forms of beauty.

Sonnet 12:00

Whether to Pedro or José, to Pepê or Juan,
You are precious to lose and you are too young to leave:
You, whose aggression sparks up to protect everyone
Attached to your heart; you, whose shallow-mindedness
Brings laughter to those who hear; you, whose distant dreams heave
The people to aim higher. You're the point of kindness.
And this world unites to pay for what you have given;
It is not enough. It will never be enough
To equalize with your generosity linen
Of happiness in return, to do it in your name.
Yet, to find smile again will be hard in this loss tough
For smiles are pulled from you and no one will be the same.

Brother, you aren't that wise and you aren't that great
But it is you who helped towards the wise and great fate.

Sonnet 13:00

You are a lime 'twixt the fingers of Society
And the sourness of your nature pleases the milieu
To have you cut and so, to make you bleed painfully
That you'd curse the heaven and just let go of everything
In hopes it would dry up to rest both the woe and you.
But you wanted to be more than what the world's thinking.
Society tells you are just one of thousand limes,
Born in expectations to ripening the rest had,
Cuffed to the obligations the rest carries and climbs.
The Society is not you – it shouts deep within;
The rest is not you – with that belief you are clad;
And you are not a mere lime – your torn heart is cryin'.

You wanted earnestly to roll off their tight clasps
But only burst in tears, with no courage that blasts.

Sonnet 14:00

When one agrees with another, their similar views
And acts are accentuated to exist thenceforth.
When these points are agreed upon by others in queues,
They become norms and laws; and so have you sprung alive.
If people wearing one perspective make up your worth,
Why are people hell-bent to break what's in your archive?
Do you know that in truth you had sprung from the silence
Of many there beneath the feet of those who dictate?
There are maybe throngs who agree with you in full sense
But it's certain that there are throngs who agree in fear
In estrangement, incompatibility and hate.
Down with confusion when some escape from your walls drear!

Accept that passivity and silence breed you.
You perpetuate your life when defiant are few.

Sonnet 15:00

Every day Sol flinches when you show that dazzling smile
From your carmine lips which would make your father see red.
To stand before a mirror has been the longest mile
You love to take, flattered with the imitation
Of the image to every motion of your proud head;
Flaunting of your newly-shaven shins for the fashion
Of the new glossy vermillion stiletto;
And sway of your angular body with feline grace.
You best Hera, show the peacock as yours akimbo.
For what crowns is the sinews to strip bare your skin
Callused by the hostility of your uppish race.
It's time to celebrate that you did not let them win.

As you stepped out of the room with a flamboyant gown,
You dare to burn with all burning eyes in the whole town.

Sonnet 16:00

Centuries have passed and many words were born and dead
But Forever remains with its wrong definition.
Billions of lovers pose as witnesses to lead
That it is known for what it doesn't really mean.
Quadrillion times and more the word is said in passion
But it never wends towards the heart's incessant yen.
Either too short or long enough's the time together,
Forever is uttered as to gratify feelings
Of euphoria believed that nothing can hinder,
But the bitter truth pierces souls in surprise moments –
That fallacy are its millennium-old meanings.
All will nod: Forever's a misnomer that torments.

Forever must not pertain to the time's endlessness
But a period where prevalent is happiness.

Sonnet 17:00

You're a figure naked of outer particulars
But your mind's chaotic with bittersweet memories
Cascading into words which are alluring like stars.
Those words that bleed and bloom are penchants more colorful
Than how you live. You, who have seen lots of ironies
Just remain taciturn without taking arms forceful.
By your keen sense you pin similes to what befall;
With no mates near, you always speak with apostrophe;
With personification, to inanimate all;
To handle every turn without enmity or howl,
By sharp wit you use euphemism and hyperbole;
How you grasp life proves your metaphor's more than an owl.

To most people you're common a fellow to look at
But your perdurable words will drop off every hat.

Sonnet 18:00

The end of harsh lane trodden for almost a lifetime
Is the gift of a plush carpet towards the palace
Of one's faith unwavering and your love sublime.
After all, the mankind is tainted by temptation;
Their lives 'neath your mercy uncut is all a class
Where faith is forged for heaven and lost for perdition.
Through your might angels dazzle brighter than any star
But no brighter than your might that made the universe;
Against you, not a fallen angel can win a war.
In every ordeal each man has to encounter,
You are ubique, as how it's told by immortal verse,
Watching with love that outlast even forever.

Mankind is indeed of your never-ending love,
And every day it comes soaring around like a dove.

Sonnet 19:00

In the dead of the night, you take a cup of coffee
Savoring the tongue-scorchingly aromatic brown
To send in exile the spirit drunk with lethargy.
You are an apprentice whose commands are lessons
That you will plunge into bravely even if you drown
For it follows the lane of your heart's earnest reasons.
As it should, you are learning to mince well the boulders
For crap sandwiches you'll help yourself with gratitude
And you are learning to fit the armor like fathers.
Who works good and faithfully believes is rewarded;
Who cries triumphant is the one with right attitude;
And who palms face is the rest by itself deluded.

You've learned and so doing to find the one you love most.
If life forfends, then love what you find at any cost.

Sonnet 20:00

At the escritoire you retired on mid-July
When the rain gen'rously kisses the earth,
And in each flavescent book you found her being lie.
There is her Literature you had exchanged by chance.
In your hated Math tucked is her picture full of mirth.
There is hers you didn't bring back that talks about France.
There is History bearing her unint'rested view.
On the rear flyleaf of Speech written is a letter
Of blooming rose caused by her no other but you knew.
The novels side by side bookmark part of memories
Quoting the inner voices, both bitter and better.
There – a dictionary which knows she's your poetries.

Seeing earth had patiently waited but not in vain,
You hope that those books will open blank pages again.

Sonnet 21:00

Do we have to encumber Love with all these numbers?
Love is intangible whose shape is ever-shifting,
Whose roots cannot be traced by the cleverest rosters;
It is omnipresent to give life and to nurture
But must not be counted for it will appear nothing,
Can't be marked for it's not the same with the breath of Nature;
It does not count neither for it comes embrace all
Without conversion, and weave them as if they're verses
Rising from the values and sometimes letting rules fall.
Love befriends Chance but not Time, running in varied rhyme;
Chance calls for entwined patience, Time calls for boundaries;
Patience bears eternity and eternity kills Time.

So let measurement grow to define the universe,
But by its times free Love powerful and never terse.

Sonnet 22:00

Seven hundred thirty days ago you went homeward
By wayfare. Upon reaching fin'lly the town central
Left you in awe of Yule embellishment the innard;
Those vibrant moth-winged lights wrapped buildings and arbors
And you're seemingly lost in a belt galactical
'Long with red-and-green moving but non-living figures.
Searching the spirit of joy in the vivacity,
Nought's there but opulence; from a view overlooking
Distantly is dismal scene – the central town only
Was lit and the rest was a vast expanse of pitch-black.
The town's grandeur, a piece of deception was swall'wing
Folk's wit; extravagance pushes their welfare aback.

Who's seated at the throne showed the townsfolks fake richness
So they'd ne'er notice 'tis on own pocket the progress.

Sonnet 23:00

Never flying off the anxiety of falling
From your enfeebled mind while your enfeebled heart
The wish of crutch you di'n't lose never was off ebbing.
'Tis measure of heavier trust which had broken
The tendons of your intertwinedness (now, wounds still smart).
And your pride and their pride were fighting for the olden
Time's sake to re-adhere: theirs prodding, yours hesitant.
Never were your arms closed to all possibilities:
Half within proclaimed freedom total and scorn blatant,
Half within exclaimed reunion and forgiveness;
But you best knew them and so the probabilities;
And what's in between lay in the future (not mere guess).

O! Deepest down all of you wanted another chance
But you wanted best: to grow independent perchance.

Sonnet 24:00

How shameful he is to be negligent of you!
When he'd utter words he longed coating them with Their tongues
And as his words had grown long, 'Might these dreamt tongues come true';
For a score you spoke well with Uncle Sam or John Bull
And with élan re words written he rose from his gangs
While you, in his own tongue hung unhoned, trifled and dull.
He longed to sound love at the top of Eiffel Tower,
To scribble hieroglyphics beside a pharaoh's tomb,
But you, his own tongue where words began had to cower?
Now with those tongues many rose too high for him to reach;
He mourned, for he couldn't fly, inside the catacomb
Of his dreams; you'd waited for him, of you, to beseech.

May he hear that there's no lovelier than a cantata
Than any of coated with the tongue of Urduja.

Sonnet 1:43

There will never be a lovelier woman than thee.
Thine impeccable radiance bestowed by heaven,
Thy healing wings gentle but the strongest there can be,
Thy haloed head aspired by many to possess,
The glorious faith and simple love of thy heart golden –
Thou art being inches to perfection. No less
Than the truest man is worthy of thy precious hands,
The man who will make thee cry but in bliss nonpareil,
The one who will draw his sword and will scour the lands
That harm the holy vow. And it is clear as crystal
That with thee, the immortality of time is real.
The heaven's with thee which is the loveliest of all.

Thy bent lyre, pluck it with the most dulcet melodies;
Then let every man render loud of thy praises.

Sonnet 11:11

E'en beauteous of cold November's end it is.
Vanilla moon amid the sea of stars colors bright
Over the century-old suburbs of M. And this
Lofty, round brilliance brings to life shadows of the quaint
Scene. The awakening, it's not for a horror flight.
Is its worth not for the rosy hearts night-stirred and faint
Emanation of any tongue-tied heart's rose? The peace
Marked with a quixotic splendor and those quite young minds,
All moonstruck and lost, have reconciled and so will piece.
No forever will come to the two joint hearts broken
Ere their own thorns and high walls. Between them must what binds
Hearts be e'en when bullets of storms on earth have fallen.

Then everything can be withstood; then the rose will have
Odd brilliance like of the vanilla moon – all gloom's salve.

Other Sonnets

I intended an Ode,
And it turned to a Sonnet.

Austin Dobson

The Green Halls

Ystrdy:
I was a monarch back when brittle still were knees
Around my head was wrapping ring guava leaves.
So this was kingdom mine that I had ever dreamt
Where 'neath my feet was stretched floor of grass unkempt,
Where tall brown columns stood as far as eyes could see –
Those coconut trees risen high, way fly birds free;
Those mangoes gnarled with earrings yellow sweet, green sour;
Bamboos that creaked with blowing wind and bending pow'r;
With bushes, vines and even mushrooms strewn around,
So this was the kingdom great that I had ever found.
O Halls, what pleasant sight your vivid green to eyes!
O Halls, what cool a roof your boughs when hot sun cries!

O Halls, what soothing song your rustles mild to mind
Along with chirps and chirns and crow, so to unwind.

Tdy:
I am peasant now, two decades then elapsed.
Alas, on me it dawned the kingdom has collapsed.
The coconut trees vanished in the smoky air
But all that remained is the stumps decayed, and there
Astray in midst of mushroomed houses made
Of bricks, scrap metals, tarps, and trunks (hewed, nailed and trimmed.)
Those logs were mine, my ever shady pillars gone!
Bamboo and mango lived like lonely orphans new in a drear town.
My ears so miss the idylls windblown from dryad's home
And choric creatures blending did ne'er come.
The lofty golden sun, o gloats with veers so rough
For I have lost the crown, when growth went by, like slough.

And here I stood amidst the soil well-stripped of grass,
Much-fed with lots of trash, The Halls, who did harass?

At Home

1.
Asleep on a sagging cot you saw her sere age
Had been toils, half a century, her companion.
The ultimate solace, to undescriedly rummage;
A downy bedding she longs for you you long for her
Because nothing compared to hers is your exhaustion,
Albeit near point of return both have spoken never;
Those silvers in hair glisten oozing down her eyes
Wishing those bones rattling are just teacups afternoon
You both shared in the gooey seasons sprayed with green dye;
Whispers her now husky voice dulcet decrescendo
As if the hymns from your castle's running out of tune
And 'gain and 'gain you sing falteringly of this woe.

Her all's the wall that protected you from four corners;
Her all's fading which you wanted to pay with all yours.

2.
Spared so long in the spare room are your ancient tools
By, not your hands years-hardened, callous-by-days, but son's
Which never, not even once, clenched spending too much joules.
So upset are for what you think is his being
Ashamed of your bread-and-butter, or his direction
That is seemingly astray for tough man's living.
So upset are you that these ancient tools no one
Bequeaths, these very tools that reared up your family –
So this fatherly sorrow is understood by none.
But just like you your son's tacit to speak of his paln;
In truth he's grateful with these tools that helped him study
But he wants to build higher and greater for your clan.

You as a father must understand then your child's dream
For he as your child knows you from toils he must redeem.

Metaphors of the Moon

I.
O Moon, thine effulgence in the kingdom ebony
Bestowed thee throne unique amidst constellation,
Exalted upon divination and poesy;
Thine effulgence cast the world in auras divided
Into romance, mystery, dread and isolation,
Ever-changing in the calendar's wayfare ignored.
Queen of the Even Sky, envied by stars myriad,
What concealed and concealments are to be found from thee
For which thine effulgence, the Sun melts and chases hard?
Queen of the Even Sky, what's the knot 'twixt thee and Sun,
Untold by mythology and science till this day?
More it seems than thou being a rose and he a gun.

Let thine effulgence cascade to the rugged surface
Of the world and light for lost men the missing pathways.

II.
A pearl exotic in the ocean black-fathomed – a dream
Prsitine to pirates ethereal fiercely grasping;
The idol of the sirens singing their wrecking scheme.
The vixen snow-clad gracefully dancing with its pipe,
The werewolves ferocious for lavish dinner howling,
The cat nine-tailed caterwauling about hollow gripe;
Another cat, of blackest furs, will tiptoe round the night,
Their eyes enkindled and so the evil will ride,
To burn down the city and spread wide a homeless plight.
Covens of witches mutter their prayers before thee
To lay a spell, their caldrons and voodoo dolls beside,
On every creature needy and worthy of change, whoever would it be.

But blooming somewhere are mystiques grown from thy tears,
The scent of these moondrops sprays good luck lasting for years.

III.
Pearl of Heavens, a power indecipherable
Is enshrouded to thy existence and thou glowest
To clothe the world in an ambience incomp'rable.
Thou art the birth of bizarre, the mirror of tranquil.
Thou art the ward of Artemis, hunter prettiest.
But thy ward most beloved is the Earth, strong and still.
Thy being's enigma. Art thou a luminary
When this planet stumbles into its darkest hours?
Or art thou a basin of strength for the deviltry?
The scale of thy judgment is distinct from Santa Claus
And although thy pallid face is a bulb for lovers
Thou give forth rewards or punishment from extreme clause.

Thou art the clock hanging on the wall vast and concave
Of mystical phenomenon belonging to eve.

IV.
A comb, more precious than jade, any princess would love
If cut into half's thy face non-cornered, composite –
The long lost comb of Alunsina she had hung above.
A crescent, quarter of thyself, O thou becomest
Stooped, towards either of directions opposite.
A queen humbly kneeling before the Lord Highest.
Sometimes as plump as croissant, or as thin as toe nail.
Nevertheless, a crescent never forgets to smile
Even when all the stars around give up to twinkle, and fail.
Yet, a beholder bespectacled with deep sadness
Shall see of that curled lip that reverse and what is vile
Like a prisoner grudgingly waiting for decease.

As a self-unknowingly subject thou art of art,
These very hearts and all they contain to thee impart.

V.
Sometimes a silver coin well-polished, sometimes a dime.
Sallow as the skin of a woman old, bed-ridden
Or as gray as the young man shot dead in a grave crime;
Could be orange coloring the sweet corns in the fields,
Pale red like the briars in a palatial garden,
Seldom as green as the woods wild loved by hunting guilds.
Or blue as thou art described in idiom once.
What is there that lies within thee? What is thy deep core?
Not only shape changes, but hue too, in cycle runs.
Every astronomer knows 'bout these occurrences
But why numbers and points cannot fill up every lore?
Still, thou art fledged from most magical references.

And if thou aren't there what life there is on the night?
How will seas and oceans glitter into lovely sight?

VI.
Sorceress cloaking thyself behind the clouds e'er still,
Swimmer diving in and rising out the clouds fleety,
Soldier camouflaging in the vesper at thy will.
When the new boast like peacocks, then why, thou, O Moon, hidest?
Ne'er forgotten's beauty, the kind only known to thee,
By a child wistful, pray'n' earnestly (may thou grantest).
In rarity, it is chalk-white, thy radiance way up
And across the rocky, limpid brooks the unicorns
Will, with a maiden most chaste and pure-hearted, gallop.
In rariy again, it's holy white in the pall
Beaming on one chosen being for the coming morns
To supernatural feats that promise royal hall.

Pull the tides, turn the odds to the favor of needy.
Pull up the tides, never drop them back for the weary.

VII.
Night Belle, wearing gown bipolar: goodness and shadows,
Gazed at by centaurs and descendants of Cassandra
For omens and future – instrument that foreshadows.
Who is the pale silhouette pale in thy pearly face lit?
Is it, waiting with the vampire troops, Count Dracula,
Lurking behind thee – the side hidden – in utmost jet?
What secrets are buried in the darkness of that side?
What memories purl then in thy scars called maria?
Was it thy man adored but whose love in no time died?
Could the vivacity of thy fullness cover pain?
Could thy lambent light be a stifled hysteria?
What had befallen that thou feared to befall again?

Night Belle, O Night Belle, what are techniques have you mastered
That the most cunning of swindlers have not learned or heard?

VIII.
Thy light is stolen from the sun, ne'er let thee be caught!
Keepest glowing, mirrored in waters, written in verse
To prove thou deservest not be taken for nought.
Keepest traveling round the world like a conqueror.
Stayest in the perigee to show thou art colossus,
Bringest the eclipse of the Sun, a moment grandeur.
And with all's fervent hope, the next song of thy Moonness
Shall thou speak out the secrets and up the true essence
To kill each wrong rumor and to kill every cheap guess.
O Moon, a luxury of tales any bard will sing
Upon thine effulgence, splendor and existence
Because in the firmament, God made thee a-hanging.

O lovely Moon, lovelier than the loveliest all,
Forget those melancholies. From thy throne thou won't fall.

Dinner With Dolorina

I.
Tomorrow when bloody robes, masks and horns prowl at night
Will multi-flavored sweets pour from scripted dense of fright;
Tonight dates our marriage, long detached, now willowy,
And pulsate will these veins barren for touch velvety.
Minutes before summons the oaken grandfather's clock,
With my grandmother's tulle cherished did I wrap the block
Of sycamore, our first fondest roost; embezzle
With china of bisque, fries and chicken roast that sizzle,
With gobletsful of iced champagne as red as your lips,
With strewn ribbons, bleeding roses and inflamed tulips.
Seconds before summons the oaken grandfather's clock,
Before come from the mahogany door the soft knock,

Did I give the lilac candle its seasonal life
And when hugs the air its lavender breath, comes my wife.

II.
On her head, I'd like to place a crown of metaphors:
A sly thief she is riding on a swift eggshell horse;
A white vixen she is skulking through eventide rite;
And a snowy owl she is taking a silent flight.
O, what a piece of cunning trick! Might not grunt the wood
But why did not bleat the hinges? How with ease she could!
There, she stands by in her wintry ethereal gown,
Glisten the charcoal eyes in the softness like of down,
And curl the strawberry lips into a sickle moon
As thump her heels on the floor, Out of beat to my croon.
There, with impeccable feline grace she stands and walks
Trailing the carpet of petals to our night-borne talks.

First a crispy kiss and then lacy arms she gives me,
Sitting on the opposite throne of Her Majesty.

34

III.
There, my ever lovely Dolorina, She sits by
Glued to my delectable craft, wearing the same wry
Smile, awkward for hundreds of moons Of togetherness,
So ironic for her mouth is a flamboyant dress:
Bold and vibrant are its colors, blistering at midday
On eyes plain and matched, visible even darks essay;
Flowery as palatial gardens or sometimes sordid
As an old pig, raised for slaughter, Tagged with low bid;
Stitched with counterfeit or festooned with eccentricity,
Buttoned with rumors or pleated with coarse honesty.
Thus, without my thinnest fibers of astonishment,
She becomes needle to loss of one's temperament.

Rarely she bids fair to be classy or eclectic,
That rarity singles her out – Genuine, unique.

IV.
For it's her fashion that follows my heart's endless trends,
Her fabric that covers my body in twists and bends;
It's her dresses that I have been keeping as my own,
Furred or feathered, a complement of my manly crown.
Her prints and patterns and price have I memorized,
To her shapes and hues and textures am I mesmerized
From which crimson pair of theatrical curtains
A series of fiery, beautiful drama opens –
The drama we acted upon a spotlight for two
When Rotation is viscous and is rapid, too.
Yes! Shines this selfsame specialty, this very hour,
And so blossoms she more than any present flower!

Though does it not, her countenance will I still embrace
And will I throw upon delightful strokes for always.

V.
There, my ever lovely Dolorina, She sits by
Drenched in our scentful corner. (Between us, same thoughts fly.)
How can I ever forget that spark when our eyes meet,
The sheen that promises stars and heaven by its heat?
For being oath-entwined with her for near half a score,
Have I seen through those dreamy jet eyes her deepest core:
Braving in phobias, preening in insecurities,
Hardened by truth, and living by hidden charities;
That those ebony eyes Are chasms of idioms
And of poetry I love to read; of axioms
And their flaws I love to be shared with. O, she can speak!
She can speak if only she sheds her mind light to speak!

My Dolorina, How she befits the simile
To owl when breaks her pinions of immaturity!

VI.
But the left morsels of her youth Feeds mine neglected
Lurching for mysteries and wonders undiscovered;
Her eyes as have I said A potpourri of writings
Fill up the unnoticed hiatus of my readings
About connections of points in various figures
Or the surprises of seeds from The One one nurtures.
More than her mouth speaks her eyes. They are compassionate
Unlike the other which shows off. Though what is innate
To her deepest soul, let it be not stereotyped;
What is vague about her; Let it be not disliked;
For so certain I am she is a wingless angel,
Merely understood but never hearted of hell.

Stern and ambitious I am but the lingering child
In her brings me free spirit and contentment dust-piled.

VII.
Tonight glows she as lambent as the chandelier
Above. Princess is she, I am a cavalier
On the first roost we're fond of. Tonight is like last night
And will be like tomorrow in our vow's might.
"Forever does not synonymize Time's endlessness
But it means the period of prevalent happiness –
That period we shall tie up into a turning loop
Where will yesterday, tomorrow and today stoop
Before us as one – A phenomenon misnamed
But very familiar as every human have dreamed.
There, my ever lovely Dolorina, she sits by.
I am terribly afraid to wave this night goodbye.

There, my ever lovely Dolorina, she sits by.
I never extremely want to wave this night goodbye

VIII.
Then thunders bellow a brief duet of start and fear,
Tap my soul from mooning to reminding the dear
Roost, the last that is the best, that lift us in the pink,
Shade similar to the candle that fell on the brink.
Off its holder my startled arms brushed the stick lilac.
The light is killed in the now solemn, decrepit shack;
The table is blank and grimy like the cracked platter
Standing under the broken bulb. Sooty smells shatter
The freshness of October wind blowing from the hole
Of the tin windows. No syllable, neither vowel
Did I utter when I glanced next at the bamboo chair.
Gone is Dolorina, and her gown, lips eyes and hair.

The call of the old grandfather's clock I didn't hear
But in the dismal silence she whispers in my ear.

About the Author

R. Speegz was born in the Land of Salt, Pangasinan. He loves language and literature, and if he has his way, he wants his career a part of his creative writing (not the other way around). He also loves hot soup, beautiful scenery, and musing under the moon.

Speegz lives in a bungalow with his father whom he bequeathed his love for music and his mother whom he bequeathed his love for poetry, keeping a stack of dark, lonely poems and chapter ones.

Printed in Great Britain
by Amazon

30258351R00022